Christianity: The Evidence

Roger Forster
& Paul Marston

Cover design, setting and illustrations by Joseph Laycock

Printed and bound in Great Britain
by Cambrian Printers, Aberystwyth

www.pushpublishing.co.uk

Contents:

Commendations

This is a book to savour. Not only do the authors provide strong evidence for the truth of Christianity but they also reveal their passion for personal knowledge of God in Christ. Make no mistake: this is not an arid work of apologetics but an intelligent commitment to Evangelism that challenges many of the assumptions of secular thinking.

Canon Dr Andrew Walker
Emeritus professor of Theology, Culture and Education,
King's College, London

If you want a clear, succinct and reasoned case for Christianity, look no further. Forster and Marston have delivered!'

John Gallacher PhD AFBPsS CPsychol FFPH
Professor of Cognitive Health, University of Oxford

Marston and Forster summarise and engage the basic claims and questions over which many stumble when confronted with self-confident secular fundamentalist who point to science as the death-knell of Christian belief.

Coherent, clear, concise and compelling as always, their book is both a good read and a structured approach that catalyses discussion and offers a short compendium of distilled answers.

You will have to conclude that it's impossible to escape the pages without recourse to belief: either there is a plausible, personal God, or not – the choice is yours, but you will understand now that either position stands or falls on faith as much as fact, save that only one can be true. As a famous media acquaintance of mine says: 'On balance, I think Jesus is who he says he is.' I happen to agree. I wonder, will you?

Professor Rob George,
King's College, London

Introduction

Key Questions

- Is faith just an irrational leap?
- Does it matter whether or not Christianity is true?
- What evidence for it is there?

Introduction

Is Faith Irrational?

Those who are not themselves practising Christians may have various attitudes to the issues of Christian faith and truth. Some think that it may be nice to have some kind of faith, but that faith is an irrational leap in the dark – believing things for which there is no evidence. Some militant atheists go further, claiming that religious faith is based solely on what people are told to believe (ie authority) rather than any evidence, and that all religion is simply irrational superstition. No distinction is made between Christian faith and a belief in tooth fairies. They claim that only science is rational and objective and that it stands in opposition to faith. Christians too may differ as to how far the facts of their faith can be 'proved'.

So has science really disproved God, and is faith irrational? Is science really about *proof* whilst faith is just about *belief without evidence?* In this book we show that neither of these claims is true.

Actually, absolute proof of anything is rarely if ever possible. Science is based on a complex set of interconnecting laws and assumptions which make generalisations about our experience. But modern thinkers about the nature of science (or 'philosophers of science') are usually 'critical realists'. They believe that science describes real phenomena but does so using human language and perspectives that are subject to amendment as science progresses.

Can anything be absolutely certain? Descartes, who is said to have laid the foundation for rationalism, began with 'I think therefore I am' – what I *know* with *certainty* is that I exist. Ironically, the atheist Richard Dawkins, famous for attacking faith as irrational, does not accept even this – rejecting any idea of a knowing 'self' in favour of the brain as merely a kind of parallel processor. Paradoxically, then, he believes there is actually no one there to 'know' and yet that science produces certain knowledge.

Rene Descartes

> ## 'I think therefore I am'
>
> — *Descartes*

So if even Descartes' core certainty of his own existence can be doubted, then surely absolute 'proof' is rarely if ever possible? But what we *can* do is try to base our beliefs in both science and religion on *evidence*, and the aim of this book is to investigate the evidence for Christian faith. We aim to show why it is important to decide whether Christianity is true, and also that Christian faith is rational and based on good evidence.

Is faith blind?

Around the world, Christian faith inspires many people, both in their personal fulfilment and in how it leads them to help others. So isn't it enough just to say that it's nice for them that they have something to believe in, even if it is irrational, and leave them to get on with it? Not really. Christians, and indeed everyone else, should believe that both *faith* and *truth* are important.

Albert Einstein wrote: "Science without religion is lame, religion without science is blind". We could paraphrase this to say: "Truth without faith is lame, faith without truth is blind."

If a person has some kind of faith which is irrational and not based on truth then they are delusional, and such blind faith might even be dangerous. It is important to note that for Christianity the claim made by the writers of the New Testament is not that what they are saying is just nice or comforting or inspiring, but that it is true.

> ## 'Science without religion is lame, religion without science is blind'
>
> — *Einstein*

But on the other hand, simply believing Christianity is true isn't the same as *faith* – it does not make someone a Christian, nor does it ensure they will live their lives in the radical way that Jesus taught. Mere belief without appropriate action is lame. Being a Christian means being in a faith-relationship with God through Jesus, which transforms us from within by the Holy Spirit. But that relationship cannot be based on make-believe, it must be based on truth for which there is evidence, otherwise it would be blind faith.

Why is it important to decide if Christianity is true or not?

Does God exist? And if so, what is God like? These are two of the most important questions people will ask at some point in their lives. Whether there is bacterial life on Mars, or whether there really was a King Arthur with a round table might be interesting to know, but will not change our basic perception of who and what we are. However, whether or not God is real affects our view of some key things about us and our human condition:

 Purpose: Was the universe created and planned by a Creator with a purpose, or is it just a great big accident, unplanned and pointless?

 Personhood: If we have been created by a personal God (ie who has personhood), then being a 'person' has special significance. If there's no God, then our personhood is merely a side-product of purely accidental movements of physical atoms, and is at best an accident and some would say a delusion.

 Morality: Morality relates to us being personal beings. But if there is no personal Creator-God, and our personhood is an accident, and without especial significance, then how could there be any real meaning or value in words like 'right' and 'wrong'? Why should they apply to humans any more than to hyenas or spiders? This does not mean that atheists never behave morally, just that it is hard to see any rational reason for them to do so. At best morality is reduced to the personal convenience of a social contract or the obscurity of a Kantian argument based on valuing the rational.

 Future: If there is no God and we are accidental by-products of a purposeless physical universe, then there is no ultimate future for us either as individuals or as humanity. Our individual consciousness ends in death, and life on our planet will end when the sun starts to expand from a yellow dwarf star into a red giant in some 5 billion years.

So by implication we can see that belief in God forms the basis of purpose, personhood, morality and hope for the future. This explains why Christianity, with its belief in a loving God, can be personally inspiring and give meaning to life.

However, critics often claim such 'purpose' is really just a crutch to prop up people's emotional insecurities or give them a warm-and-fuzzy feeling, so it is important to ask the question, "Is Christianity true?" "Is there any actual evidence for it?" Even committed Christians may sometimes wonder: "Is my faith really based on truth or am I deluding myself?"

We have noted that it is almost impossible to have absolute proof of anything, but it is sensible to ask whether there is good evidence for the truth of something if we are basing our lives on it. We do this for example in entering a career or marriage – we can never be sure of all the facts or outcomes but as far as possible we try to base a rational decision on known evidence.

So what kind of evidence is there that Christianity is true?

In this book we will look at three types of evidence for the truth on which Christian faith is based:

Nature: Does our physical universe point towards God? In Part 1, we will argue that the complexity and fine balance of creation does seem to cry out that it was designed and is not 'self-explanatory'.

History: Is there any evidence from history that backs up Christianity? If God exists and is interested in humankind, it makes sense that God may have communicated with us. Part 2 looks at the historical picture of Jesus in the New Testament, how it fits coherently into a pattern that runs through the whole Bible, and how the New Testament seems to be confirmed by historical evidence.

Experience: All human beings experience consciousness, many say they have experienced God and some claim to have seen miracles. It is reasonable to ask if these experiences point to something beyond the purely physical, and we will look at this in Part 3.

Paul's Evidence

It is interesting to note that in the New Testament, the apostle Paul also appeals to each of these three types of evidence to support his arguments for Christian faith.

In Romans 1, Paul says that nature points to a creator God who is interested in how we behave:

> '. . . what may be known about God is plain' *because* 'since the creation of the world God's invisible qualities – his eternal power and divine nature – have been clearly seen, being understood from what has been made . . . (v19-20)

When Paul speaks in 1 Corinthians 15:3–8 of what Christians believe is the key event in human history, the resurrection of Jesus, he appeals to history in the then widely-known eye-witness evidence about the resurrection appearances of Jesus. What makes this the more remarkable is that some key events in Jesus' life seem to have been prophesied centuries earlier (Acts 26:20).

Finally Paul appeals to experience when speaking of his own profound personal religious experiences, starting with his famous vision of a light and the voice of Jesus that led to him becoming a Christian (Acts 9:3–7).

So the apostle Paul saw each of these three lines of evidence as important, and we will now explore each in turn.

Discussion questions:

The sections in this book could be used as a basis for a housegroup discussion series. Leaders may want to make up their own discussion questions, but here are some suggestions:

- What difference does it make to the human situation if there is a personal creator-God or not?

- What difference to the value of being human does the existence of a personal creator-God make? Who decides what are 'human rights' and how?

- What difference does/would being a Christian make in your life?

Part 1: Evidence from Nature

Key Questions

- Has science disproved religion?
- Does nature point to a God?
- Is there purpose in the universe?

Evidence from Nature

Why are we here?

Why are we here? Why does anything exist at all? For millennia humans have searched for explanations to try to make sense of the fact that we exist, and to understand how we fit into the universe. But why do we ask these questions? Why are the answers important?

Throughout history, humans have consciously developed the use of *language* to represent the organisation and relationship of the physical world around us – structured language reflects our desire to be conscious of order in the universe. Humans have also experienced '*purpose*' - creating a plan in our minds and then acting to fulfil it by changing the physical world. To 'create' a new kitchen, for example, means planning it in one's mind before it exists in the physical world. Finally, as humans we have an awareness that physical reality seems to follow patterns or '*natural laws*'.

Is the universe due to God, or to chance?

So, applying our experience of language, purpose and natural laws to the world around us, the question has arisen: is the apparent order and purpose we see in the universe due to the plan and design of a personal creator God, or is it all due to purposeless chance? This has been a debate throughout history. The choice has always been there: is the universe due to God or to chance? (Strictly speaking, of course, 'chance' is not an agent but an assertion that there is *no* agent causing order and direction. But the choice is still real.)

How can we go about finding out the answers?

Does science have all the answers?

Science is the study of how the universe works and comprises a set of interconnecting explanatory ideas and theories (or paradigms) with varying degrees of certainty. There is no clear-cut distinction between 'laws', 'facts' and 'theories', and what constitutes 'evidence' for a particular idea is determined within the science itself. Scientific paradigms are judged on whether they make overall sense of what is observed, but often they contain unobservable concepts. Occasionally a whole set of such paradigms can be radically changed, as when it was decided that the earth orbited the sun or when Einstein's theory of relativity was accepted. We are likely in the future to see great changes in astrophysics when a theory about 'cold dark matter' is eventually established. As mentioned in the introduction, science is not about absolute proof.

There are, however, sets of scientific paradigms for which there is overwhelming evidence. So for example, taken as a whole there is evidence in a lot of areas for the general picture that the earth is about 4.5 billion years old, and good evidence for the evolutionary development of animal life over millions of years. But science only answers *what* and *how* questions – it does not answer questions about purpose and meaning. This is not because it just hasn't got there yet, but because this is not its subject matter. Some very famous scientists have recognised this.

Historically, in contrast to what is often popularly portrayed in the media, Christian faith has never been in conflict with science. Not only is the idea that great scientists were persecuted for their science a myth, but when religious persecution was rife great science figures like Johannes Kepler were actually protected by those in the opposite religious camp. This is explored in our earlier book *Reason, Science and Faith*, in Paul Marston's book *Great Astronomers in European History* (2014), and books by Allan Chapman like *Slaying the Dragons* (2013). There have, moreover, been many committed Christians who were key to the development of *all* modern sciences, including physics, geology, chemistry, biochemistry, genetics, neo-Darwinian evolution, astrophysics and cosmology, to name but a few.

Johannes Kepler

Many of the most famous scientists in history, such as Johannes Kepler, Robert Boyle, Isaac Newton, Michael Faraday and Clerk Maxwell were devout from the time of their teenage years, and in modern times Francis Collins, the man who led the team who mapped the human genome, had abandoned an earlier atheism to become a Christian in his late 20s. We personally know professors and leading researchers at top universities in physics, astrophysics, psychology, geology, paleo-biology, genetics, materials science, chemistry, ecology, etc, who combine their fervent commitment in science with an active Christian faith. But they recognize that science has limits, and it answers 'how' rather than 'why' questions. Some non-Christian leading scientists have recognized the same thing, as we can now consider.

The limits of science

Albert Einstein, the most famous scientist of the twentieth century, wrote:

> The scientific method can teach us nothing beyond how facts are related to and conditioned by each other . . . knowledge of what is does not open the door directly to what should be. One can have the clearest and most complete knowledge of what is, and yet not be able to deduce from that what should be the goal of our human aspirations . . .
> *Ideas and Opinions* (repr 1995) p. 41.

Professor Stephen Hawking, author of the best-selling book *A Brief History of Time* and one of the best-known living scientists, wrote:

> . . . even if there is only one unique set of possible laws, it is only a set of equations. What is it that breathes fire into the equations and makes a universe for them to govern? . . . Although science may solve the problem of how the universe began, it cannot answer the question: why does the universe bother to exist? I don't know the answer to that.
> *Black Holes and Baby Universes* (1994) p 90.

Though Hawking has changed his mind a few times, most of us recognise that the subject matter of science, however successful, is only part of reality. For meaning, plan and purpose, we need to look elsewhere. These kinds of question are the subject matter of theology and philosophy.

Science, mystery and observation

Science is based on observation, but often it suggests the existence of things that cannot actually be observed to explain things that can. So for example, things like magnetism, static electricity, radio waves and quarks cannot be directly 'observed' – but their effects can.

Moreover, some things are mysterious or even counterintuitive, going against what we might think seems obvious. For example, light is made up of photons and these have some features of particles and some of waves, astrophysics says that 95% of reality is undetectable cold-dark energy and matter and that there may be other dimensions and universes.

However, the weird, mysterious features of modern physics and astrophysics make it easier to believe in, for example, the mystery of the Trinity, the existence of a spiritual dimension and the reality of the Kingdom of God. When once we interviewed the Nobel prize-winning astrophysicist Sir Anthony Hewish he actually said: "It's easier to have faith right now than to believe in modern physics." But many people do not know about this aspect of science.

> 'It's easier to have faith right now than to believe in modern physics'
>
> – *Sir Anthony Hewish*

Science raises design questions

So there are limits to what science can explain and it also contains mysteries, but it may furthermore raise some questions that are outside its field to give answers. In particular, science raises some basic issues relevant to the question of whether or not the universe has been planned and designed:

1) Why does the structure of matter enable inhabitable universes to form?

Various fundamental physical constants seem to be very 'fine-tuned' to allow the formation of chemical elements as we know them. Elements essential to life - like carbon - are 'manufactured' inside stars from lighter elements. Very, very, precise 'coincidences' of energy levels in helium-4, beryllium-8, carbon-12, and oxygen-16 are needed for carbon to form without it all turning into oxygen. Cambridge Professor of Astronomy and Astronomer Royal Martin Rees, and popular science writer John Gribbin, (neither of them Christians) state:

> This combination of coincidences, just right for resonance in carbon-12, just wrong in oxygen-16, is indeed remarkable. There is no better evidence to support the argument that the Universe has been designed for our benefit - tailor made for man.
>
> *Cosmic Coincidences* (1990) p. 247.

Rees and Gribbin go on to say there are: 'at least two other striking coincidences that help to make the Universe a fit place for life.' So for example, if one of the four fundamental forces in nature (weak interaction) had been very, very slightly different, then the stellar production and distribution of essential heavier atoms could not have taken place. In this case we could not have been here. Rees' later book, *Just Six Numbers* (1999) points to the six basic constants in physics, all of which need to be within precise limits for an inhabitable universe to be possible at all. Since Rees wrote this there have, of course, been discoveries in physics (like finding the Higgs-Boson) but nothing to change his basic point.

Martin Rees

2) Why is this universe inhabitable?

Since the Belgian scientist-priest Georges Lemaître first put forward the idea in the early 1930's, the standard belief of scientists has been that the universe began with a 'big bang'. But, even

Georges Lemaître

given suitable fundamental constants, a big bang along the lines of present scientific theory could have produced a great number of different universes. The vastly overwhelming proportion of these would be either a series of black holes or have matter spread out thinly and evenly. In none of these could life exist. Professor Paul Davies is a physicist, a popular writer in the UK and USA, and is not a Christian. He has estimated in various books that for every time a big bang produced a universe there would be an unimaginably small chance of getting a universe where life were possible (see for example, *The Goldilocks Enigma* (2007)).

The renowned physicist and futurist Freeman Dyson famously remarked:

> As we look out into the Universe and identify the many accidents of physics and astronomy that have worked together to our benefit, it almost seems as if the Universe must in some sense have known that we were coming. (Quoted in *The Anthropic Cosmological Principle* (1986) by John D. Barrow and Frank J. Tipler, p. 318)

3) How did life actually originate?

Supposing that a big bang produced a universe in which life were possible. Suppose also that, among the millions of planets which are scattered throughout it, some happened to have the very, very precise conditions needed for life to exist. What would be needed for life to begin, and how often would it come about by 'chance' if not designed?

The problem is that it is all extremely complicated. Proteins cannot be synthesised without DNA (or RNA), but you cannot make DNA without proteins to act as catalysts to synthesise the building blocks of DNA. A standard university text WH and DC Elliott *Biochemistry and Molecular Biology* (4th Edn 2009), p.13 says there is:

> . . . a chicken and egg problem; which came first, protein to catalyse reactions or nucleic acids to direct the synthesis of primitive proteins?

Their expanded suggestion, in terms of an RNA world predating the development of DNA, still remains speculative. Suggesting that life formed when organic molecules arrived here from outer space only moves the problem one stage out. At present there is conjecture but no real plausible scientific theory about how life originated. Maybe one day there will be such a theory, but it is nowhere near there yet, and it requires an act of faith to assume that it will one day be found.

Science, then, *can* tell us that the odds are incredibly small that a 'chance' universe would be inhabitable, and we would evolve in it. But as to why there *is* such a universe, and whether there was a *purpose* in it (and us) coming into being, these are not even questions that science can address, let alone answer.

Christian Views of Origins

All Christians believe that God designed, created and upholds the physical world. All Christians are 'creationists', but they differ on how God did it:

1. **Young earth creationists:** believe it was all done in 144 hours maybe some 10,000 or so years ago – although they believe all the systems of ecology changed dramatically a few hours later when the first humans sinned, to give rise to the present system of nature which is savage and predatory.

2. **Evolutionary creationists:** believe that God used a process of evolution to develop all organic life over millions of years.

3. **Intelligent Design (ID) creationists:** believe that God intervened miraculously at key points in the history of evolutionary development.

We have little sympathy for the young earth view though it is held by many of our sincere fellow evangelical believers. Contrary to what 'young-earthers' sometimes claim, the timescales and neo-catastrophism (ie that there have occasionally been disasters wiping out much of organic life) which characterise modern geology were *not* developed to attack the Bible, but devout Christians like the evangelical Cambridge Professor of Geology Adam Sedgwick (1785-1873) were key in their development. In evolution, Darwin's contemporary key American supporter Professor Asa Gray was an evangelical Presbyterian, and the key figure in developing 20th century neo-Darwinian evolution,

Cambridge Professor R. A. Fisher, attended chapel regularly at Cambridge and sometimes preached. Any notion that geology and evolution were developed to attack Christian faith is simply not true. There is more on this in our book *Reason, Science and Faith* (2000). The evidence is overwhelming that the earth is ancient (around 4.5 billion years old), and that landforms and mountain ranges have changed over many millions of years due to plate tectonics. Geology, geophysics, astrophysics etc all point to this – and Christians have been amongst key figures who developed these sciences.

Moreover, the Biblical literalism adopted by young-earth creationists is *theologically* mistaken. It was *not* the classic approach of Bible-believing Christians throughout history and its modern origins come through Seventh Day Adventism in the early 20th century, not the mainstream of Christianity. Influential Christian thinkers throughout history, like Origen, Augustine, the scholastics, Calvin, Francis Bacon, key Puritans, John Wesley, the major early twentieth century 'Fundamentalists', and many others, were clear that it was mistaken to try to derive science from the Bible, and the key Christian developers of modern science all took this view.

Even more importantly, Jesus himself continually used language in a symbolic and metaphorical, ie non-literal, way – for example:

- being 'born again' (John 3:3)
- having 'living water' (John 4:10)
- having 'food to eat' (John 4:32)
- 'destroying the temple' (John 2:19).

Both his friends and enemies often misunderstood this, and the teacher and theologian Nicodemus in John 3 is gently teased for not understanding the use of symbolic language! The Genesis creation account speaks of a serpent in Eden, and in Genesis 3:15 God prophesies enmity between the descendants of the serpent and the descendant of the Woman. When Jesus refers to this he takes the descendants of the 'serpent' to be his human opponents, not a set of snakes (see Matthew 12:34; 23:33; and John 8:44). The 'serpent' is not literal, but pictures the spiritual opponent of God: *the satan* (Revelation 12:9; 20:7). Jesus and the New Testament writers were not biblical literalists. Paul Marston looks at this in detail in his book *Understanding the Biblical Creation Passages* (2010). Young-earthism also implies that the present natural world, with all its savagery, is so far removed from God's original creation as to be unrecognisable – and this is in contrast to the Biblical books of Job and the Psalms which see the present nature as God's creation (see for example Psalm 147:9; Job 38:39-41).

Jesus plainly taught that God operated *through* natural processes, such as feeding the birds (Matthew 6:36). It makes sense, therefore, to believe that God operated *through* natural processes in creating animals – Genesis 1:11 may even hint at this by saying 'let the earth bring forth...' Certainly some Christians (like the Cambridge professor of palaeontology Simon Conway Morris in *Life's Solution*, 2003) have argued that the whole system is set up so that organisms like us will arise – it is not 'chance'. Some leading modern scientists who are devout Christians like Denis Alexander, Francis Collins, RJ Berry, and many others have taken the evolutionary creationist view.

Simon Conway Morris

Frances Collins

ID creationists differ in that they believe that some organisms show 'irreducible complexity'. They say that just as to have a successful mousetrap you need *all* the parts present (spring, catch, base and bait), so some organisms have features that rely on a number of parts each of which would be useless if developed separately. The ID argument is that this shows God must have changed the normal cause-effect evolutionary process at this point in order to produce more advanced organisms. This evidence, they say, *proves* that God was directly involved, whereas ordinary cause-effect evolution does not. When ID creationists put forward any such supposedly 'irreducibly complex' organism, of course, critics then spend great effort in devising largely speculative ways in which the different elements of a structure *could possibly* have developed independently for some other purpose and then been adapted.

But we should emphasize that ID creationists also believe that design is shown in the whole system of nature. One of us had a long friendly conversation with one of its founders Michael Behe and he was adamant on this: divine design is not only in the 'gaps' in the train of scientific cause-effect, but manifest in the whole system. Though we think it a bit linguistically confusing to use the same word 'design' as (he claims) a 'scientific' term as well as a metaphysical one, his basic point is that an apparent injection of information from outside the normal natural cause-effect is a more forceful indication of divine involvement. A biochemist, Behe does not claim to derive his science from the Bible, nor does he believe the earth is young. Another leading ID creationist, William Dembski, in *Intelligent Design* admits that in theory ID is compatible with a full evolutionary model (p. 109), but again claims that his discontinuous version *demonstrates* that God *must have* been involved. The distinguished British ID creationist, John C. Lennox, notes how many famous scientists have been Christians and evolutionary creationists and adds:

Michael Behe

> . . . the evolutionary viewpoint, far from invalidating the inference to intelligent origin, arguably does nothing more than to move it back up one level, from the organisms to the processes by which those organisms came to exist . . .
>
> *God's Undertaker* (2007) p.89

In other words, although Lennox himself believes there have been discontinuous 'jumps', he still believes that the design would be apparent even without any.

John Lennox

What is our own assessment of evolutionary versus ID creationism?

Both viewpoints accept that that there has been micro-evolution, ie small changes due to evolution by natural selection. The basic divergence is that evolutionary creationists believe that all the *major* changes have *similarly* evolved through genetic mutation and natural selection. So *did* macro-evolution occur purely 'naturally' or not?

Lennox rightly points out the militant 'new atheists' often present absurdly invalid arguments for it. Actually the fossil evidence for *purely* natural macro-evolution is not conclusive. There remain large gaps in the record, which are generally explained by some idea of 'punctuated equilibrium' ie that for long periods species have been stable but that rapid evolution happened after some kind of environmental catastrophe. This rapid evolution is said to have left correspondingly fewer fossils to show it.

To us (though we make no claim to expertise in genetics) there does seem to be some good though circumstantial *genetic* evidence for macro-evolution – that is, to show that major changes have come through genetic mutation amongst organisms with common descent.

Having said this, we remain open to the possibility that there *have* been *some* scientifically inexplicable 'jumps' in organic development as ID creationists suggest, even though they are difficult to prove because some 'natural' explanation *could* always be found in the future. But if there *are* such jumps then it may be that at these key points there has been some input of 'information' or 'complexity' from outside the physical system. If there has been, then ID creationists may be right in claiming that this clearly *demonstrates* that God has been active at these points, even though they recognise that there is design in the whole set up and throughout natural processes as well. Analogously, most Christians accept that sometimes God does things, such as miracles of healing, that cannot be scientifically explained, but they do not believe that this is the *only* way that God operates in healing.

However, even if it turns out that there have been no such 'jumps' in evolutionary development then (as we quoted Lennox above in saying) this does not detract from the overall impression that the whole system looks 'designed'. Even TH Huxley (the famously pugnacious anti-church advocate for a complete Darwinian evolution in the late nineteenth century) stated that:

> It is necessary to remember that there is a wider teleology which is not touched by the doctrine of evolution.
>
> *On the Reception of the Origin of Species*, 1887

TH Huxley

The *whole system* looks designed or 'teleological'.

In the apostle Paul's words:

> For since the creation of the world His invisible attributes, His eternal power and divine nature, have been clearly seen, being understood through what has been made, so that they are without excuse. (Romans 1:20)

It was not so much, as we quoted Freeman Dyson above, the universe, but *God* who knew we were coming - because God planned and intended it.

Is there intelligent life elsewhere in the universe? Christians throughout history have held divergent views on this issue, but what we do know is that the universe *is* set up for intelligent life and we *are* it! Astrophysics Professor Brian Cox is not a Christian and has no religion. In 2014 he did a BBC series *Human Universe*, and a *Sunday Times* article on 26th October summarised his view as:

> Humans are probably the sole masters of the universe, because the evolutionary flukes that gave rise to us are highly unlikely ever to have happened on another planet.

Brian Cox

Is 'God' a real explanation?

Finally, some have argued that for us to use 'God' to explain why the universe is as it is just adds another level of mystery, ie 'Why is God as he is?' They argue that it is 'simpler' just to accept the universe as a 'brute fact' rather than to add another thing to be explained as well. The fallacy with their argument is that we are not adding a new and un-experienced 'thing' to explain. Actually, our most direct experience is of ourselves being personal beings - so to suggest that a personal being created an inhabitable world is not to add to the number of things that need to be explained. In one sense, it actually reduces the complexity from two types of thing requiring explanation (personhood and an inhabitable universe) to one (personhood), which through Creation explains both the physical universe and the existence of ourselves as persons.

A creator-God makes sense of *all* our experience of reality, reducing rather than adding to the number of things to be independently explained.

In summary, then, science tells us a lot about our universe and how it works. The complexity of nature is awesome, and seems to demand some explanation. Science, though, cannot tell us whether it has purpose and why we are here. The Christian belief in a creator-God, whatever timescale and mechanisms God is believed to have used, makes sense of it all.

Discussion questions:

- We feel that we experience 'purpose', but is the universe as a whole without any purpose?

- Is 'design' the most sensible explanation of why the universe is so complex and looks as though it was made to allow life and for us as conscious beings to arise?

Part 2: Evidence from History

Key Questions

- Why should Jesus be important?
- Is there good historical evidence about Jesus?
- Is there really evidence that Jesus rose again?

Evidence from History

Has God got in touch?

L et's suppose, whatever our beliefs, that there is a personal creator God, who gives us purpose and personhood, as we discussed in the Introduction. It makes sense that such a personal God who made the universe and created life, would want to communicate with his or her creation. If that is so, then we should expect that

God would have tried to communicate with humans at some point. So, the question is, throughout history *are there* any serious claims to be communications from such a God?

Actually, there are not many.

Many 'folk' religions in Africa, South East Asia, China and Japan are 'animistic': they believe that animals, plants and inanimate objects possess a spiritual essence. Their religion concerns the day by day appeasing of innumerable spirits, and although they may somewhere have a 'high god' or 'great spirit', these religions offer little information about him, and so do not help us in a search for a revelation from a personal creator-God.

A number of other major religions are what are sometimes called 'religions of the way'. There are, of course, great differences between the respective 'Ways' of Hinduism (Dharma), Buddhism (the eightfold path) and Taoism. In Hinduism, for example, the Bhagavad-Gita emphasizes devotion to deities in a way foreign to the others. What they share is a lack of emphasis on the personhood of the individual, and parallel to this a lack of strong identity of a personal creator-God. The individual does not seek a right relationship with a personal and just God, but 'enlightenment' implying either personal extinction or absorption into some kind of universal.

None of these religions contains clear claims to communication from a personal creator-God.

The three major faiths which *do* make such a claim are Judaism, Christianity and Islam.

So what about them? One of the most immediately striking things is that the man Jesus of Nazareth is associated in a vital way with all three! We therefore have to ask this central question:

Who was Jesus?

The three main 'one-God' faiths: Judaism, Christianity and Islam take different views of Jesus.

- The first Christians were Jewish and accepted Jesus as Messiah, but the later Jewish Talmud presents Jesus as an executed 'sorcerer', a *bad man*. (*Babylonian Sanhedrin* 43a).

- The Muslim Qur'an sees Jesus as an important *prophet*, but not divine. It also states: "…they [the Jews] killed him not, Nor crucified him, But so it was made to appear to them… No, God took him up to Himself." (*Sûrah* iv.157). So according to Islam, Jesus was not crucified.

- The Christian New Testament presents Jesus as the Jewish Messiah and a prophet, but also the 'Word of God' or 'Son of God' in human form, who *died for the sins of the world* (John 1:14; 3:16) and was resurrected to defeat death (1 Thessalonians 4:14).

So what is the real truth about who Jesus was? There are two main lines of evidence we can look at:

1. Historical coherence

Jews, Christians and Muslims all accept that God spoke to the Jewish people throughout the centuries before Jesus and that they were to expect a 'Messiah'. The most amazing prophecy of this Messiah was in the book of Isaiah, written some 400–600 years before Jesus. It pictures at length a coming servant, a chosen one, a Messiah. But what *kind of* Messiah was he, and what would he do?

Isaiah 53 says:

> He is despised and rejected by men, a man of sorrows and acquainted with grief. And we hid, as it were, our faces from him; he was despised, and we did not esteem him.

> But he endured the suffering that should have been ours the pain that we should have borne. All the while we thought that his suffering was punishment sent by God.

> But because of our sins he was wounded, beaten because of the evil we did. We are healed by the punishment he suffered, made whole by the blows he received.

> All of us were like sheep that were lost, each of us going his own way. But the Lord made the punishment fall on him the punishment all of us deserved.

> He was treated harshly, but endured it humbly; he never said a word. Like a lamb about to be slaughtered, like a sheep about to be sheared, he never said a word.

> He was arrested and sentenced and led off to die, and no one cared about his fate. He was put to death for the sins of our people.

> And they made his grave with the wicked - but with the rich at his death, because he had done no violence, nor was any deceit in his mouth. Yet it pleased the LORD to bruise him; he has put him to grief. When you make his soul an offering for sin, he shall see his seed, he shall prolong his days, and the pleasure of the LORD shall prosper in his hand. he shall see the labour of his soul, and be satisfied. By his knowledge my righteous Servant shall justify many, for he shall bear their iniquities.

> Therefore I will divide him a portion with the great, and he shall divide the spoil with the strong, because he poured out his soul unto death, and he was numbered with the transgressors, and he bore the sin of many, and made intercession for the transgressors.

The text given here is virtually identical with the scroll 1QIsa dating from about 125 BC and found in the Dead Sea area in 1947. No later Christian 'tampering' is possible. But in it God clearly says that his Messiah will come to die for our sins, not  just to be 'taken up' and escape death as most Muslims claim. Moreover the Messiah was not to come as some kind of conquering hero as some Jews expected. He was not merely to be a good man and prophet, his death was part of God's plan, for him to die for our wrongdoing. Yet, at the end of the passage, we find him the other side of death, victorious, as could only happen through some kind of resurrection.

When we compare them with the gospel accounts of the crucifixion, a number of Jewish Old Testament passages such as Isaiah 53 contain prophecies with amazing details of Jesus' actual death.

Written one thousand years before Jesus, Psalm 22 reads:

> My God, my God, why have you forsaken me? [Jesus quoted this on the cross] Why are you so far from helping me, and from the words of my groaning? O my God, I cry in the daytime, but you do not hear; and in the night season, and am not silent . . .

> But I am a worm, and no man; a reproach of men, and despised of the people. All those who see me ridicule me; they shoot out the lip, they shake the head, saying, "He trusted in the Lord, let him rescue him; let him deliver him, since he delights in him!"

> Many bulls have surrounded me; strong bulls of Bashan have encircled me. They gape at me with their mouths, like a raging and roaring lion.

> I am poured out like water, and all my bones are out of joint; my heart is like wax; it has melted within me. My strength is dried up like a potsherd, and my tongue clings to my jaws; you have brought me to the dust of death.

For dogs have surrounded me; the congregation of the wicked has enclosed me. *They pierced my hands and my feet;* I can count all my bones. they look and stare at me. *They divide my garments among them, and for my clothing they cast lots . . .*

I will declare your name to my brethren; in the midst of the assembly I will praise you. You who fear the lord, praise him! All you descendants of Jacob, glorify him, and fear him, all you offspring of Israel! . . .

All the ends of the world shall remember and turn to the Lord, and all the families of the nations shall worship before you. For the kingdom is the Lord's, and he rules over the nations.

Again this Psalm was contained in part of the 1947 Dead Sea scrolls find, and the scroll 5/6HevPs confirms the amazing words 'they have pierced my hands and feet'. The whole Psalm does not seem to relate to any experience of the person who wrote it, but it does fit perfectly with the experience of someone who was crucified and who rose again.

2. Quality of Sources

The Jewish *Mishnah* was based on oral traditions but only written down towards the end of the second century, and the *Talmud* much later. These are unlikely to be more accurate than first century accounts.

The Muslim *Qur'an* was claimed by Mohammed to have been given to him by the angel Gabriel in visions up to the time of his death in 632 AD. He was illiterate and had to memorise it. The version we have today was set down in Arabic by Uthman the third Caliph (653–656), and all other circulating versions destroyed. Its accounts of Jesus contain very few historical or geographical details of the times to demonstrate their authenticity (and any details that *are* present could easily have been reproduced from hearing them from the gospels).

This is all in contrast to the four gospels which are the first four books in the Christian New Testament, and which were written early and contain a wealth of archaeologically and historically verifiable details about the times they report – as we shall now explore.

- **Writers:** The four gospels were all written in the first century under the guidance of those who knew Jesus and who he chose to be his disciples to take his story to the world.

- **Manuscripts:** There are large numbers of early copies of the gospels. These include the third century Chester Beatty Papyrus 1 (found 1931), the late second century Bodmer Papyrus P66 and P75 (found 1956) and the double sided *early second century* Pap457 fragment of John (found 1935), which one of the present authors has seen with his own eyes in the John Rylands Library in Manchester. Copies of the New Testament are far more numerous and early  than those which tell us, for example, about the famous Roman Julius Caesar. There are many books and websites on this, see for example http://carm.org/manuscript-evidence.

  There are differences between these numerous manuscripts but these are nearly all trivial copying errors.

- **Other Copies:** The New Testament is quoted so extensively by early Christian writers from the first to the fourth centuries that virtually all of it would be recoverable from these quotations alone. By the third century, translations of the New Testament had also been made into Latin, Coptic and Syriac.

- **Knowledge:** Modern archaeology shows that the gospels all show detailed knowledge of the politics and geography of that time. Luke, for example, gets no less than 15 Roman Governor titles right (praetors, asiarchs, tetrarch, lictors, proconsul, procurator, first man etc.), and correctly notes geographical details which he could not have known at a later date. John also has geographical details which could be known only before the Romans destroyed Jerusalem in 70AD. These have to be accounts dating from the first century.

- **Historical Approach:** Gospel writer Luke tells us how he set out to compile a reliable account of the important events of Jesus' life much as any historian would - using proper sources and eyewitness accounts. The accounts of Jesus in the Qur'an date to over 500 years later and are gathered from Mohammed's visionary experiences. The gospel writers compiled their accounts from first century sources - *as history*. They were, like all historians, *selective* in what they wrote, but they didn't make bits up or rely on visions.

- **Early Dating:** Scholars don't entirely agree on the dating of the gospels, ie when they were first written. To us the evidence seems to point to all of them being written between about 45-75 AD - though it is possible that the final compilation of Matthew or John may have been a little later.

Comparison with Myth and Legend

Many societies have their legends and folk myths, for example in England we have the legend of Robin Hood. Maybe there was a thirteenth century figure on whom it is all based, who lived as an outlaw in Sherwood forest. The earliest references we have are in ballads dating from a century later, and it is two centuries before we get much of substance. His girlfriend Maid Marion came from a quite different legend and was linked with Robin in the sixteenth century. King Arthur is another such shadowy figure, supposedly from the early sixth century but for whom the first references are in the ninth–tenth centuries.

Luke

All this strongly contrasts with the accounts we have of Jesus. The New Testament writers were not just story tellers – they insisted that the events described really happened and that they saw them:

Luke 1:2 – 'Reports of these things were handed down to us. There were people who saw these things for themselves from the beginning and then passed the word on. I myself have carefully looked into everything from the beginning. So it seemed good also to me to write down an orderly report of exactly what happened.'

John 1:14 – 'The Word became a human being. He made his home with us. We have seen his glory. It is the glory of the one and only Son.'

21:24 – 'This is the disciple who gives witness to these things. He also wrote them down. We know that his witness is true.'

2 Peter 1:16

We told you about the time our Lord Jesus Christ came with power. But we didn't make up stories when we told you about it. With our own eyes we saw him in all his majesty.

Other historical evidence about Jesus

Surviving works from first and second century Greek, Roman or Jewish writers are few – but those there are refer to Christ and Christians much as we would expect.

The earliest reference to Jesus is by the Jewish historian **Josephus**, who wrote *The Antiquities of the Jews* in Greek around 93AD. The present Greek versions of his work were preserved by Christians, and contain a passage, which may have been edited later, but it probably originally read something like this:

Josephus

> At this time there was a wise man called Jesus, and his conduct was good, and he was known to be virtuous. And many people from among the Jews and the other nations became his disciples. Pilate ordered him to be crucified and to die. And those who had become his disciples did not abandon their discipleship. They reported that he had appeared to them three days after his crucifixion and that he was alive. Accordingly, he was thought to be the Messiah about whom the prophets have recounted wonders.

This is the text of an Arabic version found in 1971. If you are interested in the reasons for taking this as indicating the original text see our book *Reason and Faith* pp 65-66.

Pliny the Younger

Pliny the Younger was a Roman Governor who wrote to the Emperor Trajan around AD 110–113. He wrote of the Christians that they met on a certain day very early 'when they sang in alternate verses a hymn to Christ as to a god' and bound themselves to a high moral conduct. *Epistles* x 96–7

The Roman historian **Tacitus**, writing shortly after, described how Nero tried to shift the blame for the great fire in Rome onto a group of people 'known as Christians'. He adds:

> They got their name from Christ, who was executed by sentence of the procurator Pontius Pilate in the reign of Tiberius. *Annals* xv p 44

Tacitus

So what do we know for sure about Jesus?

- He was a first century Jewish man who claimed to be the Messiah, the Son of God and Saviour of the world.

- The four gospels were written under the guidance of his close followers and record his teachings.

- His followers claimed to have seen him perform miracles.

- He was crucified and his followers claimed he came back from the dead.

So who was he really?

Opinions differed about him even when he was alive:

1. **A Madman**:

   Therefore there was a division again among the Jews … And many of them said, '*He has a demon and is mad. Why do you listen to Him?*' Others said, 'These are not the words of one who has a demon. Can a demon open the eyes of the blind?' (John 10:19–21)

2. **A Prophet**: Some said he was like John the Baptist or a prophet like other prophets Elijah (Mark 8:27–38). But yet no other person thought of as a prophet (even including, say, Buddha, Mohammed or Ghandi) made the kind of claims that Jesus made about himself.

3. **The Messiah:** Some thought he was Messiah - the unique rescuer sent by God to save humanity. But what *kind of* Messiah?

4. **The Saviour and Son of the Living God:** 'For God loved the world so much that he sent his only son, that whoever believes in him should not perish but have eternal life.' (John 3:16)

We need to remember the amazing claims Jesus made about himself:

- He said: 'I am the way, the truth and the life, no one comes to the Father except through me.' (John 14:6)

- He said he could forgive sin (Matthew 9:6; Mark 2:10; Luke 5:24)

- He claimed he could give those who followed him eternal life (John 10:27)

- He claimed that he never did anything wrong (John 8:46)

Because of his amazing claims for himself, Jesus does not really leave us the option of believing him to be 'just a good man'. Either he was what he claimed, or he was crazy or he was evil. CS Lewis, a famous Christian Oxbridge Professor, summed it up: 'Bad, mad or God?' Yet if Jesus was bad or mad how would he teach such a high gospel of love – unless love itself is madness?

The Miraculous

For most historical accounts, our assessment of their degree of truth does not depend on whether we believe in the possibility of the miraculous. Did Sir Walter Raleigh really place his cloak in a puddle so that Queen Elizabeth I would not dirty her shoes? Probably not, but our decision either way does not involve whether or not we believe in the miraculous. Did Jesus really cure leprosy and raise a little girl from the dead? Well eye witness accounts say he did, but our decision may well depend on whether or not we accept the possibility of the miraculous.

Hasn't science disproved the possibility of miracles?

- Science is the exploration of regular cause-effect sequences in the natural world. It finds that, for example, women do not have baby sons unless there is a male sperm to fertilize their eggs. Mary and Joseph, and Luke who records the events and was a doctor by trade, clearly know that normally virgins never ever have baby sons.

- But Christians believe that the physical world is only one part of reality. If, as we believe, it was created by and is kept in existence by a spiritual God, then a belief that 'miracles' can happen is perfectly reasonable. A comparison would be a computer programmer setting up a 'virtual world' on a computer and letting it run. This would normally run in a certain way, but there is no reason that its designer could not sometimes alter things in it.

- If Jesus *really is* who Christians believe he is, then his doing miracles is not surprising. Indeed, the New Testament writers saw these miracles as 'signs' (though not proofs) that his claims were true.

- Finally, it should not be thought that Christians believe miracles only happened in Jesus' day. Christians today sometimes see healings that cannot be explained by science, because the same God is at work today. In fact, science makes us more certain that something outside the usual cause-effect sequence has happened because we can be more certain of correct diagnosis. Both the present authors have personally experienced such healing miracles.

So we are left with having to decide who Jesus really was. Was he just a 'good man' and a 'prophet', or was he the unique son of God who died for our sins and in whose life we see the marks of someone more than human?

One of the biggest claimed miracles, of course, was his resurrection from the dead, and we will look at this next.

Discussion Questions: Evidence from History

- If there is a creator-God would he want to communicate?

- Where can we look in history for such a communication with humanity?

- Was Jesus bad, mad or God?

Evidence for the Resurrection

In normal terms, the whole idea of a resurrection would seem ridiculous. The death and resurrection of Jesus 'makes sense' only because it is a part of a whole plan of a personal creator-God to deal with the problem of sin and to offer us eternal spiritual life.

So what is the evidence?

- A group of Jesus' close friends and followers, dispirited after his execution, claimed to have seen and spoken to him over a period of about six weeks after his death.

- These followers were otherwise apparently honest and normal people, of all kinds of characters and backgrounds.

- They were prepared to die for their claims and most did.

- Their beliefs were reflected in Early Church teaching, and in the gospel accounts compiled around 15–50 years after Jesus' death.

Let's consider some different ways in which people have sought to explain the gospel accounts without accepting that a resurrection really happened. It may be helpful for you the reader to first read through the four gospel accounts, and also to have these available to hand for the following sections. The relevant chapters are Matthew 27:57–28:20, Mark 15:42–16:20, Luke 23:50–24:53 and John 19:38–21:25.

Was it all a mistake?

The gospel accounts record Jesus being taken hurriedly after his death to a nearby family tomb. Could it just be that Mary Magdalene and the others went to the wrong tomb early on the first Easter Sunday, and the story became a rumour before anyone could correct it?

There are two really big problems with this theory:

1. The tomb belonged to a man of importance in the community: Joseph of Arimathea. Also present was a Jewish council member Nicodemus. Such men of standing and integrity would surely have denied any untrue rumours and simply produced the body.

2. The authorities, moreover, would surely have known the location of the Jerusalem family tomb of a council member, and would have produced both tomb and body to stop the rumours.

Was it a fraud?

There are three very obvious problems with the idea it was a fraud:

1. Jesus and his followers taught a very high moral code – surely, then, fraud and deception could not really be at the centre of their message?

2. The claims to have seen Jesus by significant numbers of people mean that (unless they were unusually easily fooled) a large number must have been involved in the cover up if not in the plot.

3. If it were a fake, how can we explain the courage and boldness of the small group of demoralised disciples so soon after Jesus' death? How can we explain their being ready to die for a lie?

Was it a hallucination?

Did all those who saw Jesus simply hallucinate? Again this idea has some key problems:

1. There were apparently lots of different types of people involved, with very different characters, and at different times of day.

2. They actually did not seem to expect a resurrection to happen. The women went to the tomb to anoint the body - not to see if Jesus had risen. The first accounts of the women were received with disbelief.

3. Why didn't the authorities produce the body? Why invent the story that it was stolen?

Is it all a legend?

Legends often spring up about remarkable individuals. In British legends King Arthur pulled a sword out of a stone block and Robin Hood married Maid Marion. In Chinese legend the spirit of the drowned poet Qu Yuan asked people to use three cornered rice packages to ward off a dragon. If the Gospels were written down long after Jesus' death, couldn't they be full of legends? There are four main problems here:

1. As we have noted, legends arise years later but the gospels were written soon after Jesus' death - the first perhaps as soon as fifteen years after.

2. All the very earliest references, including early Christian writings from the late first and early second century, refer to Jesus' death and resurrection.

3. The actual accounts seem to contain a lot of detail and incidental corroboration.

4. Anyone making up a legend would surely have invented an 'eyewitness' version of Jesus emerging triumphantly from the tomb, or a dramatic first meeting with Peter. The gospels record neither.

None of these alternative suggestions really make any sense.

Do the four resurrection accounts fit together?

To Christians the crucifixion and resurrection of Jesus are the key events in human history.

Do the four gospel accounts of the resurrection fit together in a way we would expect if each is based on eyewitness accounts?

39

Any detective or judge knows that honest and genuine eyewitness accounts of any lengthy event will all differ. People can be in different places and so see different bits of an overall pattern. Different people will record different bits - noticing different details or skipping for dramatic effect over particular details.

The first three gospels have a lot of material in common because ancient authors did not see anything wrong in incorporating good and reliable sources in their historical work without citation. However all four gospels contain a different resurrection account. In each case, on this so crucial event, the gospel compilers each used the direct testimony of their main source. The gospels do not carry any authors' names, but the Early Church has left us a good idea of the main authorities behind each one, and we see no reason to doubt this:

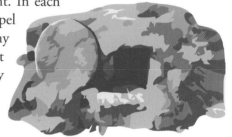

- **Matthew** reflects some input from the disciple Matthew Levi, a former tax collector.

- **Mark** reflects the preaching and viewpoint (as early church writers state) of Jesus' leading disciple Simon Peter (this is reflected in a quotation in Eusebius' *Ecclesiastical History* iii. 39).

- **Luke** contains a more general compounded account made by a Greek Doctor who accompanied Paul (see I Howard Marshall: *Luke: Historian and Theologian*, 3rd Edn, 2006). Whilst in Jerusalem for a couple of years around 58AD Luke may have spent time with Jesus' mother and some of his disciples.

- **John** was compiled within a church tradition based on 'the beloved disciple' (John 21:21–24) and the Early Church identified this man as Jesus' cousin John Zebedee who was one of the 12 disciples. Modern scholars do not all agree on this, but the evidence for it seems good to us – even if some of the gospel's final form was shaped by later concerns. As already noted, it is strikingly accurate on the geography of a Jerusalem that was totally destroyed in 70AD and it is John Zebedee whose resurrection account is recorded in it.

One criticism levelled at the resurrection accounts by people wishing to denounce them is that the four resurrection accounts are not only different, but are actually contradictory. However, by carefully reading the texts it is possible to fit all the four accounts together without contradiction and with some incidental corroboration.

Locations after Jesus' Crucifixion

Jesus was arrested in Gethsemane, an olive grove just East of Jerusalem city. Most of the disciples (apart from Peter and John) ran away from the city, going to Bethany which is about 1.5 miles in the opposite direction. There they stayed during Jesus' trials and crucifixion. The place of crucifixion was Golgotha (Calvary) and the tomb is believed to have been nearby.

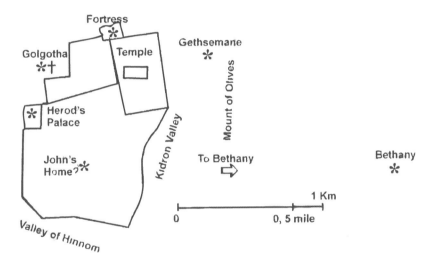

After the crucifixion, John seems to have taken Jesus' mother Mary straight back to a home he owned or rented in Jerusalem (John 19:27). Peter, after his well-known triple denial of Jesus, also went back to John's home – where he is found in John 20:3. Other women who watched the burial (Luke 23:55) also probably went back to John's home. These included Salome (the sister of Jesus' mother, also probably the mother of James and John) and the 'other Mary' who was married to Cleopas (or Clopas – probably Jesus' uncle). Mary Magdalene would also naturally have stayed with them, but Joanna (as wife of Herod's Steward Chuza) went to the nearby palace.

Mary the wife of Cleopas, and Salome, both had sons amongst the disciples at Bethany, and Mary Magdalene may also have had relatives there so they would have wanted to exchange news (John Wenham's book *Easter Enigma* and our book *Reason and Faith* present the evidence that Mary Magdalene was actually the same person as Mary of Bethany the sister of Lazarus and Martha - this helps, but is not strictly necessary for our reconstruction.) If they set out around sunset the next day then the trip could be done without breaking the Sabbath which restricted how far they could travel. These two Marys (maybe with Cleopas) walked to Bethany. They stayed there overnight.

Early next morning, Matthew 28:1 (giving the point of view of Matthew who was at Bethany) records how the two Mary's set out *'towards dawn'*.

They went back to John's house in Jerusalem, where they were joined by Salome and (according to Mark 16: which reflects Peter's view) they went on to the tomb *'as the sun was risen'*. Luke, with his more global picture, implies that they were joined on the way by Joanna who would have been staying at the nearby palace.

Meanwhile, Matthew implies, the guards at the tomb understandably fainted at sight of a shining angel, who rolled back the stone. They then recovered and ran off before the group of women arrived. It is important to note that *no one saw the actual resurrection*. Had these writers simply been making it up then surely they would have put in a dramatic account of the actual event.

When the women did arrive at the edge of the tomb garden, Mark makes it clear that they were some way off when they saw that the stone *'which was very large'* (16:4) had been rolled back. What did they conclude? John 20:2–3 tells us that Mary Magdalene concluded the body had been taken, and at that point ran back.

✝

We should note how the different accounts fit together:

1. It is *John* who tells us that *just from seeing the stone* Mary Magdalene jumped to her conclusion that the body had been taken, and it is *Mark* who tells us that they saw it some way off *'because it was very large'*. Together this explains why Mary Magdalene did not see the angels at this point. By this time (as Mark and Luke say) the angels were inside the tomb, and Mary jumped to her conclusion and ran back before actually reaching the tomb or looking inside it.

2. John (unlike the other Gospels) has mentioned *only* Mary Magdalene going to the tomb. But note what she says after running back to his house: 'They have taken the Lord out of the tomb and *WE* do not know where they have laid him' (John 20:2). This contrasts with John 20:13 where she has by then lost contact with the other women and so says '*I* do not know where they have laid him.' John 20:2 recorded the plural 'we' because that is actually what she said – and it was seared on John's memory. But it really 'makes sense' only in the light of the other accounts.

This kind of fitting together is exactly what we might expect if they are all partial but true accounts, reflecting genuine events.

Now two things happened at once. The other women went on (recorded by Matthew, Mark and Luke) to have a conversation with two angels who were by now inside the tomb. Angels are shown on Christmas cards and paintings with wings, but in the Bible they always simply look like men. Luke refers to them as 'men' (24:4), but later as 'a vision of angels' (24:13). There is no contradiction. Likewise Matthew and Mark mention only one angel, while Luke mentions two. Perhaps only one spoke, and Matthew and Mark don't think it necessary to mention his companion.

Meanwhile, Mary Magdalene delivered her message to Peter and John, who rushed off to the tomb and found it empty. The other women returned to John's house where they waited for Peter and John to get back, and then told their story about the angels. Among the hearers were Cleopas  and his friend, who set off to Emmaus - as recorded by Luke. Their conversation on the road (Luke 24:13–33) shows that they knew exactly what the women, Peter, and John, would have told them. Mary Magdalene, having delivered her news to Peter and John, went off back to the tomb – missing both the other women and Peter and John on the way – and had her encounter with Jesus himself mentioned later in John's gospel (John 20:11–17).

Meanwhile, the angels had given the other women a message for 'the disciples'. Having given the message to Peter and John back at John's house, they were running towards Bethany to tell the rest of the disciples when Jesus himself met them (Matthew 28:9). Matthew's gospel records the meeting with Jesus immediately after the meeting with the angels - just as Matthew himself heard it recounted when the women arrived at Bethany.

So, we can see that by piecing the accounts together from these different points of view, we end up with a complete story that not only makes sense, but is corroborated by various incidental details.

If the accounts fitted any easier together, or if they all included exactly the same details, then we might suspect collusion. As it is, they do indeed look like accounts with input from different eyewitness sources. They certainly do not look like legend or fantasy. Either an ancient novel writer has cleverly constructed the four separate accounts or else they are independently compiled records of genuine events.

But the four gospel accounts were compiled in different church traditions in different places. There is no way that someone could have cleverly constructed them to look like inter-relating accounts.

There are, then, some key things to note about the four accounts:

- On two key issues, things in one gospel become clear only in the light of things in another:

  1. John says Mary Magdalene ran back when she saw the stone, Mark says this was when they were some way off, which explains why she did not see the angels.

  2. John switches from '*we* do not know where they have laid him' (20:2) to '*I* do not know where they have laid him' (20:13) – this makes sense only because we know that initially Mary was with other women at the tomb, though John mentions only Mary.

- The first people to see Jesus were women, and the angels gave the women a message to tell the men what to do. This is very un-Jewish, and no Jewish writer would have made up a story like this.

- There is no claim that anyone saw the moment the stone rolled back and Jesus (presumably) came out. There *are* dramatic accounts like this but they are demonstrably late-second-century forgeries.

So overall we can see that the gospel accounts, rather than being contradictory, combine together to make very clear and reasonable case of evidence for the resurrection of Jesus.

Can we prove that Jesus rose from the dead?

Of course not! How can we *prove* it? What would such a proof *look like*?

As we look at the evidence we also have to remember that a resurrection makes *sense* only if Jesus really was who he said he was. If he were merely a man then his coming back to life after being crucified would make no sense – when you are dead you are dead and a person crucified by the Romans was *very* dead. But if he really is the unique Son of God - the Word of God become human - then it does make sense that death could not hold such a being and he could come back to life.

Is the evidence convincing?

A number of famous people have started out disbelieving the resurrection of Jesus, but after studying the accounts have become convinced of its truth.

One famous example is the journalist Frank Morison, who was skeptical regarding the resurrection of Jesus, and set out to analyze the sources and to write a short paper entitled *Jesus – the Last Phase* to demonstrate how it was an untrue myth. In compiling his notes, he came to be convinced of the truth of the resurrection, and set out his reasoning in the book *Who Moved the Stone?* Many people have become Christians after reading this book.

Many other intellectuals, often lawyers, have written similarly throughout history. For example in the eighteenth century Gilbert West and Lord Lyttelton were lawyers who set out to write disproving the gospels and resurrection and both became Christians. In the nineteenth century another lawyer Dr Simon Greenleaf wrote *An Examination of the Testimony of the Four Evangelists by the Rules of Evidence*. In the late twentieth century law professor Norman Anderson wrote *The Evidence for the Resurrection*. The young agnostic Josh McDowell started out as he was preparing for legal studies to write disproving Christianity, and finished up becoming a Christian and writing many Christian books including *The Resurrection Factor* (2005) and *Evidence for the Resurrection* (2010).

Discussion Questions: Evidence for the Resurrection

- Does any other explanation than an actual resurrection make sense?

- If the four accounts are not reports of genuine events, how can we explain the way in which they fit together?

- If it were really a carefully made up story, would all the disciples have been prepared to die for it?

- If Jesus really did rise again from the dead, what would it mean for you?

Part 3:
Evidence from Experience

Key Questions

- Is our experience of the 'self' just an illusion?
- Can people really experience miracles?
- Is religious experience 'just psychological'?

Evidence from Experience

Who am I?

As humans, we are not only aware of many different sensations, such as what we feel, see, hear, smell and taste, but we can reflect upon them. We also use language in a special way, in a structure that relates concepts and includes abstract ideas. We 'think' both in our imagination and in words and sentences. We *consciously* make decisions, that is we are *aware* of doing so. All of this is implied when each of us uses the word 'I'.

Now, I may be mistaken about whether what I am experiencing is actually 100% 'real' (whatever that means). For example, a particular 'experience' might be an actual physical event, or it might be a dream, a result of drugs or a giant hologram. But what I *cannot* doubt is that there is a 'me' who is having the experience.

But is this experience of being 'me' just an illusion?

Susan Blackmore, in her 1999 book *The Meme Machine* (applauded by militant atheist Richard Dawkins) argued that the human mind is nothing more than a parallel processor, infected by ideas (or 'memes') like a virus infects a computer. There is no internal 'I' or inner conscious self. She triumphantly concludes:

> . . . even our inner conscious self and our sense of freewill are illusions created by the memes for the sake of their own replication . . . we can be truly free – not because we can rebel against the tyranny of the selfish replicators but because we know that there is no one to rebel. (p 246)

We are free because 'really' we are not there at all. This is weird. Who is the 'we' who are free if there is no one there? Who is she writing for if actually there is 'really' no one out there? How odd to charge people £9.99 to prove to them that they don't exist! None of this is, of course, to deny that our brains *are* parallel processors or that brain states and experiences do correlate. But whether the brain-mind association is seen, for example in terms of different dimensions of one reality or as in any sense interactive, our personal experience of being conscious is hard to deny. Philosopher John Searle, in his classic Reith lectures, wrote:

> I'm conscious I AM conscious. We could discover all kinds of startling things about ourselves and our behaviour; but we cannot discover that we do not have minds, that they do not contain conscious, subjective, intentionalistic mental states; nor could we discover that we do not at least try to engage in voluntary, free, intentional actions.
>
> *Minds Brains and Science* (1984)

John Searle

The Professor of Philosophy at Warwick University, Roger Trigg (now Emeritus) also noted that if there is no one to 'know' then there cannot be scientific knowledge:

> Consciousness, and the further ability to be self-conscious and reflect about one's own states, are eliminated by a scientific programme at the cost of bringing into question the very status of science.
>
> *Rationality and Science* (1993)

Roger Trigg

Most basically then, how could scientific *knowledge* be possible if there is no *knower* there to *know* it? So if science really were to disprove the reality of any 'I', that is, get rid of any being that can 'know', then there could be no scientific knowledge, or indeed knowledge of any kind.

Questions about 'me'

Whether I call it a psyche, self, or a self-consciousness, or something else, once I accept that there really is an 'I' - a personal being – there are two obvious questions I need to ask:

1. Where did 'I' come from? Does my consciousness just exist from my own body or does it have another source? Was there any personhood (an 'I') that existed before humans did?

2. What happens after I die? Do 'I' continue to exist beyond physical death?

Christianity claims to answer both of these questions.

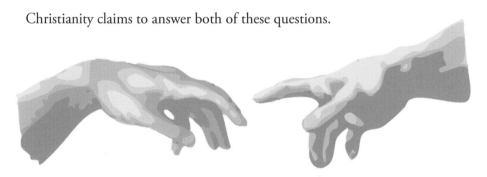

The answer to the first question is that personhood is not some accidental by-product of matter operating under blind physical laws. Rather, God is an 'I' - personhood is central to the creator God who made humans in his image. When in Genesis 1:26 God said 'let us make humankind in our image' he made both male and female in his image, but Jewish writers never took this to mean that God had two arms, two legs etc. The essence of personhood seems to be consciousness, awareness of right and wrong, love and emotions, and the capacity for complex language and inter-personal relationships. Our personhood is not an accidental by-product of matter, but a more basic kind of reality.

In answer to the second question, the survival of the person after physical death, the Bible says that those who have faith in Jesus and are in relationship with God through him receive eternal life. Death is not the end.

Miracles

In Part 2 we looked at the issue of miracles in the context of historical evidence for the life of Jesus. But miracles also form part of the personal experience of many Christians today and through history.

If we think about it, a universe with *no* regularity would be uninhabitable; it is therefore not surprising that we find regularity in the universe we are in. The methodical study of that regularity results in what we call 'science'. It involves inventing concepts and laws with which we can understand that regularity and predict future experience.

So can science tell us whether the physical chains of cause and effect are *totally* invariable? No. The success of any scientific law can be decided only by experience and observation - and experience and observation are also the only way to tell whether there are ever exceptions to such laws. We know some things are true because they are '*tautologies*' that is they are true by definition. For example, Carbon 12 always has the atomic mass of 12.00000 amu – because if something had a different atomic mass it would not be Carbon 12! In contrast, any rule or 'cause and effect' that is *empirical* is known only because we have repeatedly observed it to happen. But however many times we observe it, this cannot logically *prove* that it will always happen in the future. We construct a 'scientific law' based on experience, and whether there are any *exceptions* can only be determined by experience too. So for example it was once thought that 'all swans are white' – until the discovery of black ones in Australia. Maybe we have some inner 'feeling' that small particles may be more predictable than swan colours, but there is no strictly logical reason for this to be so. Thus, for example science tells us by experience that normally cancers cannot suddenly disappear, but it cannot logically conclude that this *never* happens, and numerous Christians have experienced exactly this after prayer for healing.

The term 'miracle' itself does not mean an inexplicable event which has no cause but one that is brought about by a different level of causality. This reflects the Christian view of reality, where (as we have seen) the physical world is dependent on God for its continuing existence. Christian thinkers have always believed this, including some of the key founders of the idea of scientific law. The founding chemist and scientist Robert Boyle, a devout Christian, is seen as the prime figure in the 'mechanical philosophy', that is the generality of scientific cause and effect. But Boyle believed that the universe only kept in existence through God's action, and that God could do and did do miracles. The apostle John writes of the divine logos who became human in Jesus, and the New Testament says of him

> . . . all things were created through him and for him. And he is before all things and in him all things hold together.
> (Colossians 1:16-17)

> . . . (the Son) . . . through whom also (God) made the worlds; who being the brightness of his glory and the express image of his person, and upholding all things by the word of his power . . .
> (Hebrews 1:2-3)

The universe continues to exist only because God so maintains it. Moreover God is seen as active within natural processes. He 'creates the winds' (Amos 4:13), and 'feeds the birds' (Matthew 6:26). But if they are his processes he can also vary them if he wishes. We looked at this in Part 1.

If Jesus was really who he claimed to be - the Son of God - then it would be surprising if he didn't do any 'miracles'. But Christians today also see many incidents in which people are apparently healed in processes that are not within the usual laws of science. In fact, science makes this more demonstrable, because the diagnoses are known with more certainty. Miracles on their own do not 'prove' Christianity, but their reality is a part of the evidence that it is true.

Religious Experiences

Many people claim to have had some form of religious experience, which has caused them to believe that there may be more to reality than our mere physical existence. These experiences happen among people of different faiths or no faith, but are especially common among Christians.

1. **Sense of awe**: Sometimes a person will experience a sense of awe or intuitive recognition that there is something behind the physical universe.

2. **Inner conviction**: Someone can have the inner conviction that God has been present with him or her in a particular situation. This can vary from a quiet conviction to an overwhelming sense of divine presence, and can happen in situations that vary from the mundane to extreme crises.

3. **Charismatic experience**: Sometimes people feel as though God is working or speaking *through* them. The word 'charisma' means gift, and it is as though God is giving them a gift to use for others. This could involve speaking in a language that the person him/herself does not know, feeling conviction that a message has been given, feeling 'anointed' in the preaching of a sermon, or being used in a physical healing (see 1 Corinthians 12:8-11).

4. **Visionary Experience**: Some people have an experience of literally seeing a vision or hearing a voice - like the apostle Paul when he saw a light and heard the voice of Jesus on the Damascus road or John when he wrote the book of Revelation. We know of people from a background unsympathetic to Christian faith who have come to faith through a vision.

5. **Experience of extraordinary 'coincidences'**: Sometimes people experience a coincidence in their lives that seems so extraordinarily improbable that they can only conclude that it is part of a Divine arrangement. Of course we realise that, for example, although the odds against winning the national lottery jackpot are 14 million to one, if 14 million people do it then one will probably win. But some of the 'coincidences' we have heard of are so unlikely that it would be like the same person winning the lottery ten times in a row!

6. **Experience in prayer**: This can involve both the feeling of experiencing the presence and love of God in prayer, and also sometimes in the kind of extraordinary 'coincidences' that happen after prayer, like point 5 above. This is not unreasonably often seen as a direct *answer* to prayer, although of course not all prayers are answered in this way.

Jesus claimed to be the only way for a person to be right with God (John 14:6). To accept this claim is to accept that anyone who has been right with God

– before or after Jesus came – has been so through Jesus. But it does not mean that all of them have heard about Jesus – and obviously Jesus was not known to faithful Jews in the Old Testament let alone non-Jews like Melchizedek and Job. John says that the *Word* (the Greek word he uses is *logos*) was the true Light which gives light to everyone coming into the world (John 1:8–10). God can speak into everyone's heart, and their experience of him is real. Don Richardson, in *Eternity in Their Hearts* (2006) has described many interesting experiences from around the world where people experienced God in this way before they came to hear about Jesus.

Assessing Experience

Could all such religious experience just be some kind of illusion; a brain malfunction, a psychosis, or a survival device of human genes?

Now obviously there are times when, for example mentally ill people may have visions or experiences that resemble those of saints in church history. But this does not prove that there are no genuine religious experiences. A comparison might be that mentally ill people may, for example, hallucinate experiences of snakes - but this does not prove that there are no real experiences of snakes. Whether my particular perception of a 'snake' is real, hallucination, or dream, has to be decided by criteria other than the pure experience itself. The question is, does that experience 'makes sense'?

Based on these criteria, the claims of many Christians to have had a personal experience of God, Jesus Christ, and the Holy Spirit, must surely count for something. Religious experiences - as a part of a general pattern of experience of consciousness and of the miraculous - make sense.

Discussion questions: Evidence from Experience

- Are you really there? Is your consciousness of 'self' real?

- Do you believe that miracles can happen?

- Do you have any experience of God acting in your life or speaking in your heart?

Response

Key Questions

- When is the best time in life to respond?
- What does it mean to become a Christian?
- How do I become a Christian?

Response

What should I do Now?

We have seen that nature, history, and human/religious experience together point to Christianity as the view of reality that makes the most sense. There is good evidence for its claim to be the truth about God, the universe and ourselves.

But 'God' is not merely the logical conclusion of a series of deductions. He is a person. The point of it all is not just to conclude something about him, but to get to know and experience him.

Decision or delay?

Christianity involves a personal commitment. There may, however, be some who, although they accept the evidence for the truth of Christianity, want to delay taking any action. Here are some of the most common reasons for delaying making a decision:

* I'm too young/too old (delete as necessary).

* I'm not good enough/not bad enough (delete as necessary).

* I'm too busy at present, I will think about it later.

* My family background is not Christian.

* I don't know all the answers and still have a lot of questions.

Jesus makes no exceptions to the need to receive him - old or young, good or bad. We take seriously the various problems and difficulties in Christian belief, but if we waited until all our problems and questions were solved then we'd never do anything about anything. Actually, when we enter into the relationship then we begin to find out more about the person.

This is true of other relationships. It is good to think, for example, about marriage before entering into it. But if we waited in hopes of one day knowing everything to know about relationships and about the other person, then we would die single.

Commitment to Christ is not 'blind faith', but it does involve a trust that there are answers to questions we may have.

Becoming a Christian

Jesus promised all those who received him the power to become the children of God, to all those who believed on his name. (John 1:12)

But how does someone 'receive' Christ? The simple message of the early Christians was 'repentance toward God and faith toward our Lord Jesus the Christ (Messiah)' (Acts 20:21).

What is repentance?

The first essential in repentance towards God is the readiness to be as honest before him and with ourselves as we are able. The second essential is a willingness to follow his plan and purpose for our lives, and to allow him to begin to change us from within, to transform us by the renewing of our minds (Romans 12:2). Repentance means turning away from a life without God to a life seeking to follow him.

Repentance is needed by all who accept God's offer of a relationship with him, but people can experience it differently. Some may feel that they hardly believe God is really there, others are convinced in their minds but have never experienced the reality of God in their lives. Some may hesitate because of the possible cost that repentance may bring.

We must not try to copy others, or expect exactly the same experience to follow. It is with this honesty of mind that we should tell God that from now on we want to go his way. But this alone does not make someone a Christian.

Faith

John 1:12–13 says: But as many as received (Jesus), to them he gave the right to become children of God, to those who believe in his name.

In Acts 16:31 Paul and Silas said, 'Believe in the Lord Jesus Christ, and you will be saved, you and your household.'

A true Christian is one who 'believes in' and 'receives' the Lord Jesus Christ. The name 'Jesus' means 'the Lord is salvation', and Joseph was told you shall call his name JESUS, for he will save his people from their sins (Matthew 1:21). The word 'Christ' is just the Greek translation of the Jewish word 'Messiah'. To 'believe in his name', therefore, is to believe that he is Saviour and also Messiah.

But in the New Testament meaning, 'believe in' does not just mean believe about, but to put faith and trust in. A sick person is not made well by knowledge about a doctor, or even by belief that a doctor can heal, but by the doctor himself/herself when the person places themselves in the doctor's hands. Our knowledge about and confidence in the doctor helps us to go to the doctor. But the point is that we must place ourselves in the doctor's hands. In the same way we may know much or little about Christ, and our confidence in him may be great or small, but the real point is an act of faith whereby we commit ourselves into his hands. It is those who actually call on the name of the Lord who are saved (Romans 10:13). This 'calling' involves being prepared to turn in repentance, confessing in prayer and asking God for new spiritual life. The confidence that Christians rightly have in their Lord may develop after this act of faith.

The Outcome

In the relationship with Christ that has begun, the new Christian should begin to read the Bible seriously, starting, we suggest, with the Gospel of John. The Bible will become a living book as God speaks to him or her through it, and prayer will become a time of real sharing.

Experiences of the beginnings of Christian faith vary. For some it is a gradual process, maybe if their family were Christians. For others it is a definite moment of decision. But for many who do make such commitment they 'feel no different', and no blinding lights from heaven shine! Experiences do vary, but often changes begin to be noticed after a time and God begins the person's transformation from within.

The Gospels record an incident that we have found to be helpful to some people during their conversion and first few weeks of Christian experience:

> Then he (Jesus) made the disciples embark and go on ahead to the other side … he went up the hill-side to pray alone. It grew late, and he was there by himself. The boat was already some furlongs from the shore, battling with a head-wind and a rough sea.

> Between three and six in the morning he came to them, walking over the lake. When the disciples saw him walking on the lake they were so shaken that they cried out in terror: 'It is a ghost!' But at once he spoke to them: 'Take heart! It is I; do not be afraid.'

> Peter called to him: 'Lord, if it is you, tell me to come to you over the water.'

> 'Come', said Jesus. Peter stepped down from the boat, and walked over the water towards Jesus. But when he saw the strength of the gale he was seized with fear; and beginning to sink, he cried, 'Save me, Lord.' Jesus at once reached out and caught hold of him, and said, 'Why did you hesitate? How little faith you have!'

> Then they climbed into the boat; and the wind dropped. And the men in the boat fell at his feet, exclaiming, 'Truly you are the Son of God.' (Matthew 14:22–33)

Was this ghost-like figure, so far removed from Peter's everyday experience, really Jesus? His doubts were resolved only after he had stepped out, and he could later say: 'Truly you are the Son of God'.

He had to act upon what he already knew, and so he started talking to the indistinct figure: 'Lord, if it is you, tell me to come to you . . .' There is good evidence for God, but many may come to him still in some doubt even whether he exists. The way to an inner assurance is through action – speaking to God and asking to come to him.

What were the thoughts that rushed through Peter's mind before he stepped out? Was it really Jesus? What would his friends in the boat think? Suppose it didn't work and he sank - how stupid he'd look! How could he face the storm, raging around them?

How many people since then have not come to Christ for fear of what their friends might think, or fear of the storms of persecution that might come, or fear that it might not work?

Peter started out, looking into the face of Jesus Christ. Perhaps he was tempted to look down at his feet to examine the great experience he was having. Had he done so then he would have begun to sink, and so lost the experience altogether. Christians too may become so involved in examining themselves to see how their experience is developing, that it begins to leave them. If we keep looking towards the face of Jesus, the experience will take care of itself. Peter saw the strength of the storm and was afraid. Sinking, he cried: "Save me, Lord", and was at once rescued. God's concern is that we should come, and if we begin to sink in fear, the Lord Jesus will save us if we call to him.

We need to keep looking towards Jesus Christ as we meet him day by day and find him in the Gospels. Leave the laughter of some friends behind us in the boat, walk through the storm, and let the experience take care of itself. Finally, a deep peace and joy in believing is left to us as we know that Jesus has come to be with us and guide and stimulate us in the adventure of Christian living.

Evidence and Faith: Discussion Questions

- What stops me/my friends from making a commitment to become a Christian today?

- If not today, then what will make me/them ready?

Response Prayer

Here is a simple prayer you could use to become a Christian:

Heavenly Father.

I am sorry that I have not come to you before, and I repent of not living in your world in your way.

Now I want to do your will.

Please forgive me for the things that I have done wrong.

I thank you for sending your son Jesus, and accept his death for all the things I have done wrong. I accept your forgiveness and receive your son Jesus into my life as my Saviour and my Lord.

I intend from this point forward to live for you as his disciple.

Thank you for the help of your Holy Spirit in leading me to this point of decision. I ask you now for him to fill me with power to live and love for you every day. Please begin the process of transforming me from within to become more like Christ.

Amen.

Further Reading

Some other books relating to the various topics are:

Roger Forster & Paul Marston: *Reason, Science & Faith* (2000)

Paul Marston: *Understanding the Biblical Creation Passages* (2010)

Denis Alexander: *Rebuilding the Matrix: Science and Faith in the 21st Century* (2002) *Creation or Evolution Do We Have To Choose?* (2014)

Francis Collins: *The Language of God* (2007)

John Polkinghorne: *Exploring Reality: The Intertwining of Science and Religion* (2005) *Reason and Reality* (2011)

John Lennox: *God's Undertaker: Has Science Buried God?* (2009)

Ernest Lucas: *Can We Believe Genesis Today?* (2005)

Stephen C Barton & David Wilkinson: *Reading Genesis After Darwin* (2009)

Rodney Holder: *Big Bang, Big God* (2013)

Craig Blomberg: *The Historical Reliability of the Gospels* (2007) *Jesus and the Gospels* (2014) *Can We Still Believe the Bible?* (2014)

Graham Stanton: *The Gospels and Jesus* (2002)

John Ankerberg & John Weldon: *The Passion and the Empty Tomb* (2005)

John Wenham: *The Easter Enigma* (2nd ed 1993)

Fraser Watts: *Theology and Psychology* (2002)

Malcolm Jeeves: *Minds, Brains, Souls and God* (2013)

James S Bell & Stephen R Clark: *Christian Miracles* (2005)

Roger T Forster: *The Kingdom of Jesus* (2014)

Nicky Gumbel: *Alpha: Questions of Life* (2003)

(A more detailed bibliography can be found on www.pushpublishing.co.uk/evidence)

About the Authors

Roger Forster has an MA in theology and mathematics from Cambridge University. He is leader of the Ichthus Christian Fellowship, and is known internationally as a preacher, speaker and evangelical leader. He has been a member of the Council for the Evangelical Alliance, Vice President of TEAR Fund, and Administrator and founder of the March for Jesus movement.

Together Roger and his wife Faith have written *Women and the Kingdom*, and his solo books include *Suffering and the Love of God – The Book of Job*, *Prayer – Living in the Breath of God*, *The Kingdom of Jesus*, *Trinity*, *Saving Faith*; *Fasting*, and *Saturday Night, Sunday Morning . . .*

Paul Marston has a BSc (Econ) and an MSc in statistical theory from LSE, an MSc in the history and philosophy of science, an MA in holiness theology, and a PhD which concerned science, methodology and Christian faith. He is a Senior Lecturer in the University of Central Lancashire. He has also spoken at conferences, Christian Unions and at Word Alive on issues of science and faith.

His solo books include *The Biblical Family, God and the Family, Christians, Divorce and Remarriage, Understanding the Biblical Creation Passages, Women in Church Leadership and in Marriage, Gay Christians and the Jesus-Centred Church* and *Great Astronomers in European History*.

Paul and Roger have co-authored a number of books including: *Yes But . . ., That's A Good Question, Reason and Faith, Christianity, Evidence and Truth, Reason, Science and Faith* and three editions of *God's Strategy in Human History*.